FIRST LESSONS
FINGERSTYLE UKULELE

BY RICHARD GILEWITZ

Online Audio

To Access the Online Audio Recording Go to:
www.melbay.com/30519MEB

Table of Contents

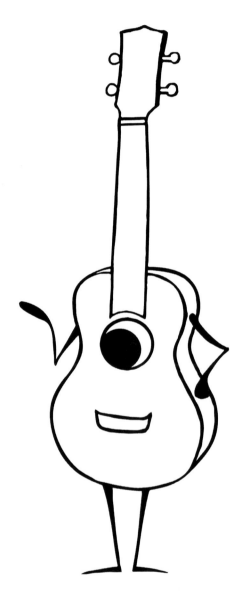

Audio Tracks

Track 1   Twinkle, Twinkle

Track 2   Bicycle Built for Two

Track 3   My Grandfather's Clock

Track 4   Oh! Susanna...Key of C

Track 5   Oh! Susanna...Key of D

Track 6   Auld Lang Syne

Track 7   Ode to Joy

Track 8   Silent Night

Track 9   Waltzing Matilda

Foreword

The Ukulele Adventure Begins

I never know what adventure will happen during my musical journeys. There are always surprises that appear in my unpredictable life. So, there was no way I could have foreseen a ukulele would become part of both my journey and career. This little member of the lute family, an adaptation of the Portuguese machete brought to Hawaii by Portuguese Macaronesia Island immigrants in the 19th century, was now going to be my new adventure.

While in the UK over a decade ago as part of a promotional tour for a guitar line based in Tacoma, Washington, I met with their overseas distributor, Mark Pugh. We spent less than a week together on a successful tour and then both said, "Adios".

Fast forward to 2014 in Buxton UK as Mark and I reunited in a local café. Mark mentioned he was now the owner of Stones Music and was distributor for a number of ukulele lines as well as innovative accessories and musical products. Our chat turned toward the idea of me helping Mark out in his new endeavor. There was just one catch. I would have to learn how to play a ukulele!

Hence, the *Ukulele vs. the Advanced Beginner Project* was born. Although I have performed on stages from New Zealand to Ireland with points in between, my 40 years of playing and years of teaching experience told me that this was an undeniably risky project to undertake, riddled with

fears, doubts, and the potential for humiliation (OK–a bit dramatic). Remember, my instruments of choice have 6 or 12 strings. I was still up for the challenge sensing that there were many elements available for effective transfer from the instruments I was familiar with to this new world of a 4-string ukulele.

The joy of this adventure extended beyond the scope of any trepidation I might have had. I was genuinely excited about the opportunity to learn and teach in a uniformly balanced exchange of techniques, ideas, and exploration of musical repertoires.

The journey began at Promenade Music in Morecambe UK. As the crowd gathered I noticed two things. Everyone who walked in had a ukulele and nobody had a guitar! Suddenly fearing that reality was upon me and wondering if I was about to meet my Maker (who of course would be a ukulele player), I hoped no one noticed I was starting to make that face similar to the person in a 50's horror film who sees the monster first.

Before I could recover my more pleasant fear-factor face, I was introduced. It was now that I had to practice what I preached to students: how to react when you screw up a performance with either a bad note played or loss of focus. The only proper thing to do is rely on training, not panic, and jump back on the escalator, train, bicycle, or any metaphor of your choice.

At the very beginning of the night I had to shift to the mindset of why I was there and to remember that this was not an event about posturing, ego, insecurity or doubt, but to share what I knew. It was the music that the evening was all about.

Fast forward two seconds and what happened was exactly what should have happened. I greeted the group, thanked them for coming and let them know just a bit about me, where I was coming from, and how I was there to both help and learn at the same time. It didn't hurt that I shared with them that it was my first ukulele clinic, which was a bit of a cheap shot to lure them into the land of pity and compassion! I let them all know that music is not supposed to be about competition. If it were, it would have been in the Olympics by now. "And in this corner, the C Major chord...and in this corner the G Major 7th flat 5!!!!!". Amusing, but honestly, how ludicrous would that be?

What I shared was all about the elements of the craft of good musicianship, communication, and an existence where the craft is improved upon in the woodshed along with extensive visits to the playground where the music is either played out or performed.

Within minutes we, as a group, were clapping out various rhythms, accenting designated beats, fingerpicking, listening to the person nearby without participating, exploring the art of visualization for both hands, and adjusting to various tempos with the guidance of the metronome, which I affectionately refer to as the *metro-groan*.

All this was done before we picked up our instruments. The group was now dialed into each other. When a series of four simple chords were applied, we had already established somewhat of a symbiotic musical relationship. The pressure was off for many folks when they realized that it was not only ok, but preferred that they didn't play all the time. This is what prevented stage fright from entering the room, gave individuals a chance to listen to what was happening around them, and to practice the art of exiting the tune followed by re-entry.

Beginner through advanced players jumped on board, sometimes with basic clapping or strumming and sometimes with improvisation from the more experienced players. As a result nobody was left out. The thought probably never crossed anyone's mind if their new beloved instructor even knew five chords on the ukulele, which was fine because we were all doing exactly what we came for: learning and having fun at the same time.

A unique feel, sound, and personality emanated with each of the four groups I taught during the tour. By the end I realized that during these clinics I had been immersed in a gathering of musicians at all levels flailing away on ukuleles, banjoleles, washboards, kazoos, flutes, and tambourines. It was the ultimate Phase 1 of the Ukulele Adventure.

About the Book

When I first embarked on the creation of this book I must admit I was both intrigued and a bit intimidated by what I was about to encounter along the way. Having played fingerstyle guitar for over 40 years and ukulele for only about two, I was curious about how many elements would effectively transfer from a 6 or 12-string guitar to a 4-string ukulele. From the start there were some obvious differences, such as fewer strings. But in fulfilling a request for a beginner's fingerstyle ukulele book, it became apparent to me rather quickly that music is music, regardless of the instrument.

Developing a repertoire based on good technique, an understanding of time values and rhythm that comprise a tune, a bit of basic theory, and some imagination in regards to creating a piece of music or embellishing/decorating a performance of a piece, these foundations all play a role in the skill development of any player.

For the sake of this book, all of those elements can't be covered. But a starter kit, including a language or system of fingerpicking patterns, basic musical notations, a handful of chords and a sensible sequence of playing these chords, along with a small repertoire of tunes (hopefully familiar to many players), should be a good jump start into the world of fingerpicking a ukulele. All of the material in this book can be played on a soprano, tenor, or concert ukulele, which are all tuned from the nose to the toes as G C E A.

Try to memorize the various chords and sequences of chords supplied in this book so that you can begin to develop your own tunes or have a better understanding about how many songs are actually structured. Accompanying each tune are chords that can be strummed simply as a background to the melody. This melody can be fingerpicked on the ukulele, played on an entirely different instrument, or sung.

Also try to memorize the tunes in this book. Although this will take some time I would recommend patience, diligence, and tenacity. The rewards are tremendous once you have actually locked a piece of music in your memory because that is when you will begin to instinctively decorate the notes and phrases with various nuances over time.

It is very tempting to be lazy and use printed music of any kind as a crutch. If you put in the effort, one day it will become apparent how the effort was actually worth it and you will enjoy watching the music grow and spring to life. I wish you the best of luck, but more than anything I would encourage you to have fun and as it's been said rightfully so a million times – enjoy the journey!

While navigating through this book, keep in mind there are many options to playing the instrument in regards to both left and right-hand fingerings. I have included only one particular way, not because it's the best way, but because it is one of the several ways to approach what I like to call *mapping out the hands*.

In the beginning you may find that you would prefer not to use your ring finger when plucking one of the strings or you might have trouble with a particular finger when forming a chord and choose another way. However, the two main things I want to point out is once you decide on one of the ways to map out the fingering choices ahead of time and program that into your hands – stick to it. I'm convinced that often it is the indecisiveness about finger position during a performance that can lead to the roots of stage fright. The element of doubt and hesitation can trigger all kinds of hiccups.

The other practice I adhere to as often as possible is in regards to picking finger substitution. I will rarely use the same finger twice in a row when plucking. Throughout this book I have mapped out some suggested plucking fingers enabling the player to avoid this double-trip hiccup which I often compare to someone who might be running and suddenly elects to use the same leg twice in a row. There are some occasions when I do choose to use the same finger twice in a row. If it is during a slower passage or a quarter note beat, it is not much of an issue.

Once a piece is mapped out properly, the fluidity that can occur allows the fingers to walk, so to speak. This preparation of proper finger placement has helped me tremendously in achieving smoothness and confidence with my playing. Believe it or not, you may even sense your body tensions are minimized and your breathing improves when the *hand planets* are lined up.

I would strongly suggest that you consider getting with a good music teacher who can enlighten you even more in regards to musical note values. This will help you to understand timing along with the extensive use of a metronome. Now that I have mentioned the dreaded metronome, I suggest that you use it in this fashion as I often do. Play a maximum of three beats with the metronome within a bar, allow for a single click, and cycle the exercise. Then expand to the full measure, plus a single beat from the follow-up measure, and then wait for three clicks to occur before returning to the cycle. Set the metronome at a much slower speed than is intended for the eventual performance level of the tune.

Best of luck to you all and once again I hope you enjoy the music, material, and journey. There is no end game – just stay on the path.

Richard Gilewitz

UKULELE ADVENTURES
A 12 POINT SYSTEM

1. *The Beginning*: Keep in mind that if you plan on becoming a practitioner of the ukulele there are two schools of thought to consider: your time in the woodshed and your time on the playground. In the woodshed you spend time improving your craft. On the playground – well, you're just having fun playing. I recommend highly you do both. If you continue to improve your craft, even a little bit at a time, you will always be satisfied. If you don't have some fun playing as well, you won't be happy. So look for a balance which does NOT have to be equal. Just keep both motors running.

2. *Technique*: I can never stress enough the importance of technique to students and players. Good technique on all fronts will grease the wheels to make everything run smoother.

3. *Transfers:* Consider your movements as you change notes and chords. Sometimes a staccato or glissando can be effective during transfers as it depends on the nature of the tune you are playing. A staccato has a stopping or snappy delivery and a glissando is a smooth ride.

4. *Note Values*: Study your timing of the various notes from whole notes to quarters, eighths, sixteenths, dotted notes, tied notes, and so on. Too often players will simply play a piece of music from a page through mimicry if they know the tune. If they don't study the correct timing, then they are clueless to the way the tune was written. I strongly recommend this lifelong practice of observing and studying timing.

5. *Rhythms:* There are so many rhythms to choose: down and up, syncopation, samba and rhumba. Once again, this is a lifelong study. Recognize there is a whole world of rhythms out there that often define cultures. As you add different rhythms to your playing, you will notice your tunes are energized.

6. *Dynamics:* This is the most fun part of playing a piece of music. Once I've gone through the steps of developing a piece to memory, I put in dynamics that will decorate the tune. I like to call them the sprinkles on the ice cream or note treatments, such as hard versus soft strikes, vibrato, or harmonic notes. All of these contribute to bringing a tune to life.

7. *Fingerpicking Patterns*: As opposed to strumming, finger picking an instrument (whether it be a guitar, banjo or ukulele) can prove to be exciting and often required for certain tunes you might look to develop for your repertoire. Just like the various rhythms available, fingerpicking patterns can be yet another musical journey.

8. *Theory:* A basic understanding of music theory can prove invaluable for a player of any instrument. It can be very easy to be quickly overwhelmed by the amount out there. I would recommend starting with just the basics, such as how a group of chords can be sequenced to play a very simple and catchy tune.

9. *Repertoire*: A collection of tunes that you can play for yourself, for others, or with others is, at least for me, the ultimate goal. Too often I've heard players who have some outstanding licks but they can't play a tune. Collect up a good batch of tunes that you have a passion for to stay inspired and always work on new material.

10. *Strategy:* I've had people ask me over the years about whether or not I have a practice regiment. I recall in the early days of my playing I was very structured, but not as much now. The only trick I can think of is to suggest you pick up your instrument and hit the woodshed AND playground every day, even for a few minutes. Also, as I like to say, put your mind on it. Think about the music in some fashion periodically throughout your day, even for a few minutes. Make music a part of your life and it will settle in to your head over time.

11. *The Human Condition*: Surprisingly players and students often forget to consider all of the elements of the human condition while practicing and performing. Try to consider your breathing, posture and various body tensions while you're playing. Attempt to play with your eyes closed and get a mental visual over time. This is especially effective when using a metronome. Easier said than done, but this is one of the most valuable points I can think of to offer.

12. *The Players*: It is very common for players to talk about other players or their favorite performer out there. I would love to just share a few of mine, but I've decided to pass. It doesn't matter. During your journey it will be unavoidable as friends, strangers, and fellow players will offer up suggestions on practically everything on a daily basis. Simply put, see what and who you like. Emulate a good player who has good technique if you wish. But in the end, develop your voice and stick with your own style.

Navigating the Ukulele and Music

It may seem counter intuitive, but as your fretting hand moves closer to the soundhole you are moving up the neck. The tone you produce goes up in pitch as you fret closer to the soundhole.

The body of the ukulele projects and amplifies the sound of the plucked strings. There is a bridge to the right of the soundhole that anchors the strings.

The neck of the ukulele is complex. It has frets and fret bars, place markers and a headstock with tuners and string posts. Tuning keys adjust the tension on the strings. Tighter tension equals a higher pitch. Always tune before you play your ukulele.

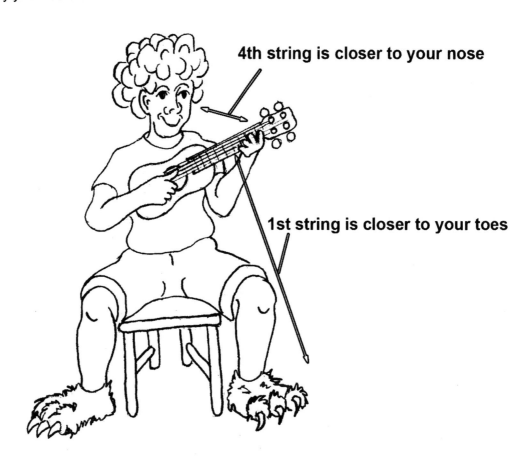

4th string is closer to your nose

1st string is closer to your toes

Standard Notation uses five lines. Vast amounts of information are shown in S.N.. Note pitches and timing value are just two pieces of information shown. As you become more serious about playing ukulele you may want to make reading S.N. a goal.

Tablature is a visual map of an instrument's fretboard. The number of lines are determined by the instrument's number of strings. Your ukulele has four strings so ukulele tablature has four lines. Notice that the tuning for each string is shown on the far left of the tablature. The numbers on the lines(strings) relate to the fret that is fretted.

Navigating The Ukulele and Music Continued

Mnemonic Devices come in handy when memorizing the tuning order of a ukulele's strings. Below you will find two examples. Use one of them or create your own.

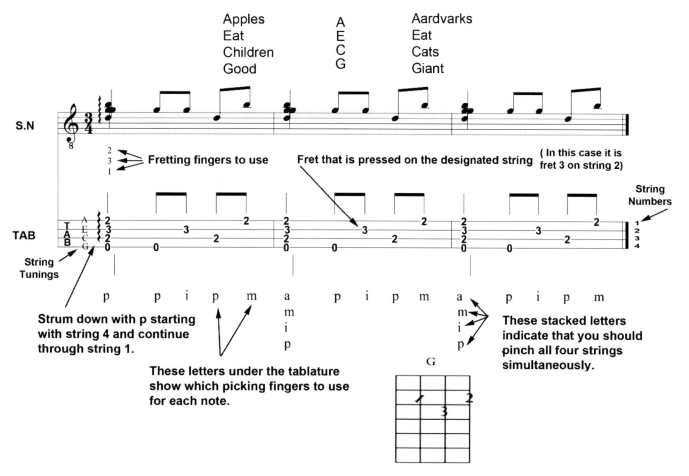

Apples	A	Aardvarks
Eat	E	Eat
Children	C	Cats
Good	G	Giant

S.N

TAB

Fretting fingers to use

Fret that is pressed on the designated string (In this case it is fret 3 on string 2)

String Numbers

String Tunings

Strum down with p starting with string 4 and continue through string 1.

These letters under the tablature show which picking fingers to use for each note.

These stacked letters indicate that you should pinch all four strings simultaneously.

Fretting and Picking Hand Legend

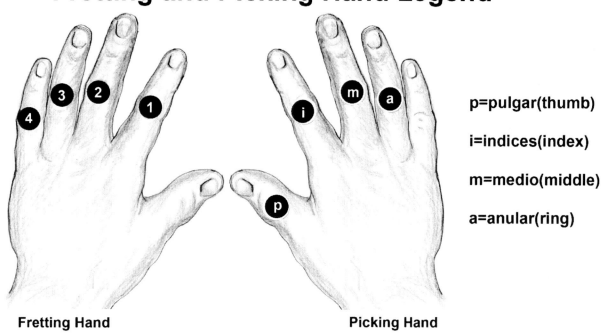

Fretting Hand

Picking Hand

p=pulgar(thumb)

i=indices(index)

m=medio(middle)

a=anular(ring)

Basic Components of Timing

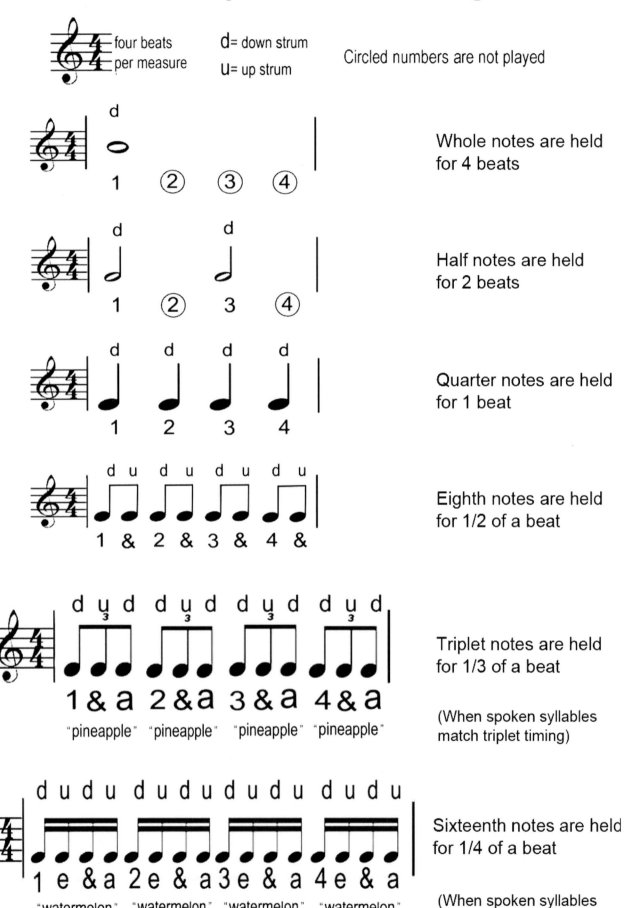

four beats per measure

d= down strum
u= up strum

Circled numbers are not played

Whole notes are held for 4 beats

Half notes are held for 2 beats

Quarter notes are held for 1 beat

Eighth notes are held for 1/2 of a beat

Triplet notes are held for 1/3 of a beat

(When spoken syllables match triplet timing)

Sixteenth notes are held for 1/4 of a beat

(When spoken syllables match sixteenth timing)

Additional Components of Timing

On the previous page you were introduced to the concept of note values. The examples were applied to measures in $\frac{4}{4}$ time. This is called "four four time" or "common time". Sometimes the $\frac{4}{4}$ is indicated by using a $\mathbf{C}$ instead of the $\frac{4}{4}$. The upper four in the symbol $\frac{4}{4}$ indicates the number of beats within the measures and the lower four tells us that those beats are quarter notes. The majority of the tunes in this book use $\frac{4}{4}$ time which is the most common timing. Two tunes "Bicycle Built For Two" and "Silent Night" were composed in $\frac{3}{4}$ the second most popular timing. Using what we learned about $\frac{4}{4}$ time we can discern that $\frac{3}{4}$ has three quarter notes in each measure.

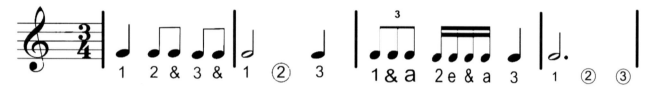

This series of measures in "three four" $\frac{3}{4}$ time uses a variety of note values. Each measure has a total timing value of three quarter notes.

Rests are spaces of silence in between played notes. They are indicated by symbols that coordinate with the value of played notes. For example a quarter note rest is a period of silence that is sustained for the value of a played quarter note.

whole	half	quarter	eighth

When you come across a rest in a measure be prepared to "silence" the sustain of the note directly to the left of rest. If you look at "My Grandfather's Clock"-Key of F(Simple) you will find examples of half and quarter note rests within the arrangement.

Dotted notes adjust the time value of a note by increasing its sustain. First you consider the value of the note, then you sustain it for a period of time that is equal to half of the notes original value.

Additional Components of Timing Continued

Let's consider an easy one, the **dotted quarter note** ♩. . Normally a quarter note equals one beat in a measure. It is also equal to two eighth notes. If a quarter note is dotted then one must increase the note's sustain by the value of an eighth note (half the quarter note's value). The dotted quarter note is sustained for a time equal to three eighth notes. The illustration below will help you visualize some common dotted note values.

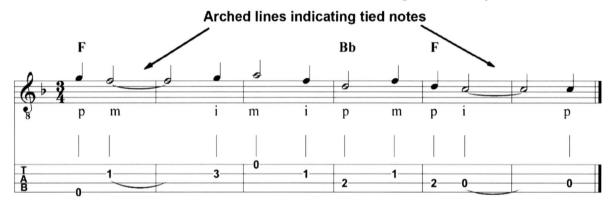

♩. = 3 eighth notes   Dotted Quarter Note

♩. = 3 quarter notes   Dotted Half Note

Skim through the provided tunes and you will find many instances of **dotted notes**.

Tied notes are also found in musical notation. Let's look at this fragment of "Bicycle Built for Two".

Arched lines indicating tied notes

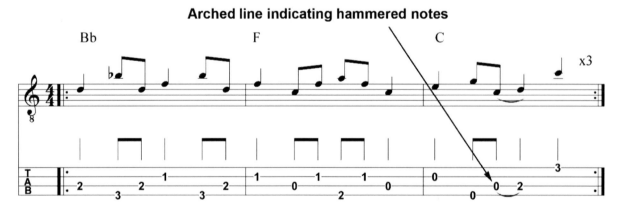

The 1st note of the tied pair is plucked and held through the value of the note on the right. The note on the right is not plucked because it matches the one on the left. In our example the left notes are half notes that are tied to matching half notes. Ultimately this results in the plucked notes being held for the value of a whole note that straddles two measures.

Arched line indicating hammered notes

In this case the notes do not match, resulting in a "hammer-on". The eighth note "0" on string 3 is plucked, then the quarter note "2" is hammered and held for the quarter note value.

GROUP 1

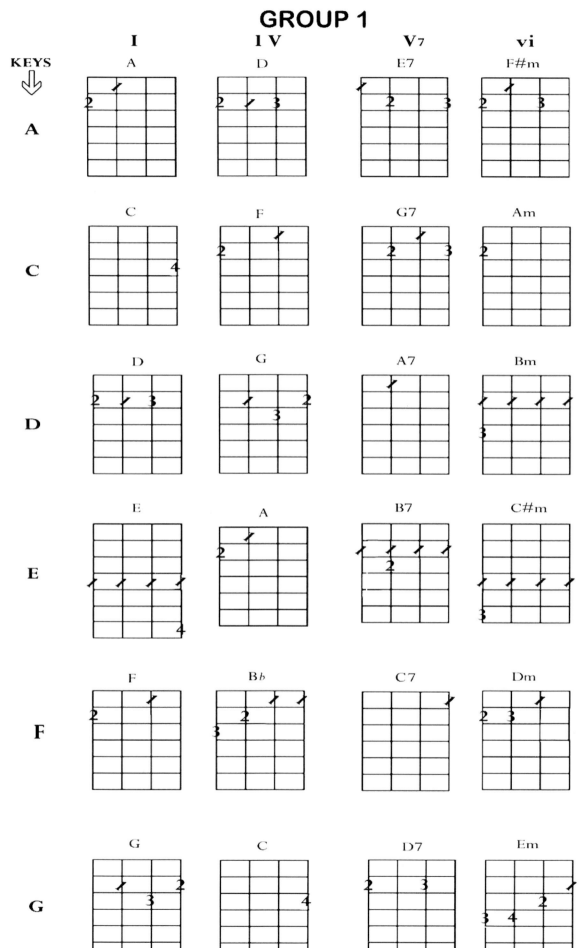

15

GROUP 2

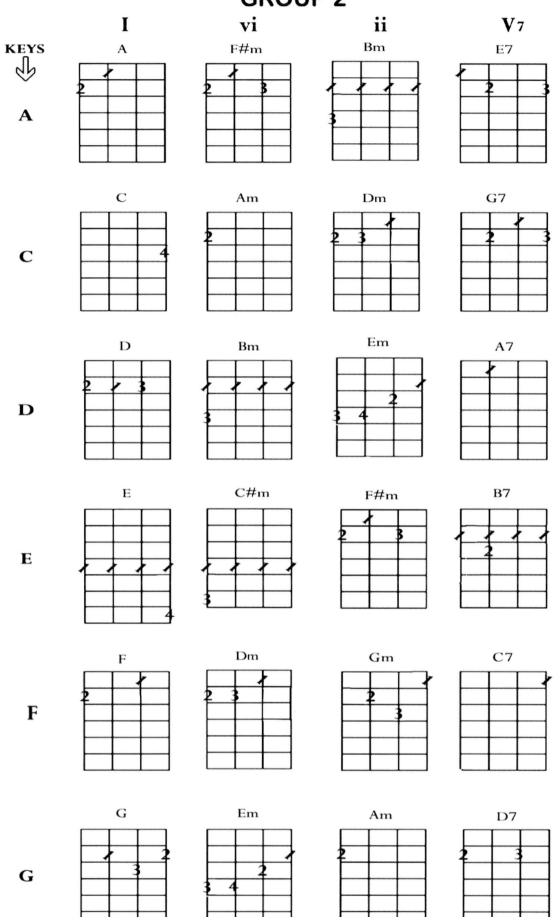

The Ukulele Fingerpicking Engine

The lines on the staff represent the ukulele strings. The *numbers* on the lines represent the frets to be played by your fretting fingers. The lowest line on the staff represents the bass string (closest to your nose!) on the ukulele. On a soprano, tenor, or concert ukulele this would actually

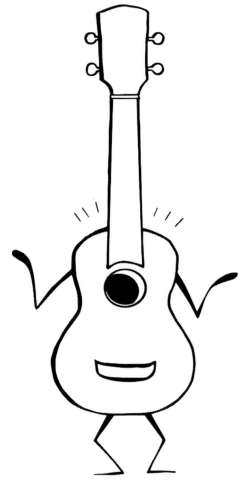

sound higher than the other strings since it is an octave string. Due to my guitar background I am used to calling the note closest to my nose the bass string. This string is often used on a ukulele to either play a melody note or for the purpose of creating a harp-like effect, sometimes during a transition or simply for effect.

The top line on the staff represents the highest or treble string (closest to your toes!). In this example string 4, which is the lowest line on the staff, has a 3 on it. This refers to the 3rd fret of the string closest to your nose. The 2 appears on the highest line on the staff, which actually refers to the 2nd fret of the string closest to your toes. This appearance on paper almost seems counterintuitive to the way the instrument is facing and is often a very common point of confusion when reading tablature. (Refer to Example A)

The 'p', 'i', 'm' and 'a' fingers represent the picking hand fingers. The 'p' is for your thumb, 'i' is index, 'm' is middle and 'a' is ring finger. I will often either set these fingers on strings 4, 3, 2 and 1 respectively or occasionally shift down and place my 'i' and 'm' fingers on strings 2 and 1. This allows 'p' (the striking thumb) to accommodate strings 4 and 3.

Another trick I use constantly is to avoid having the same finger strike the same string twice in a row. When a situation arises in the music that requires the same string to be struck twice in row, I will often borrow one of the other fingers. This allows for greater fluidity from the plucking hand. (Refer to Example B). For the *Ukulele Fingerpicking Starter Kit* I have simply placed x's on the staff lines to represent locations. Most chords can be substituted at random. For example, the 1st arpeggio with an F chord followed by a C chord would be as it appears in Example C.

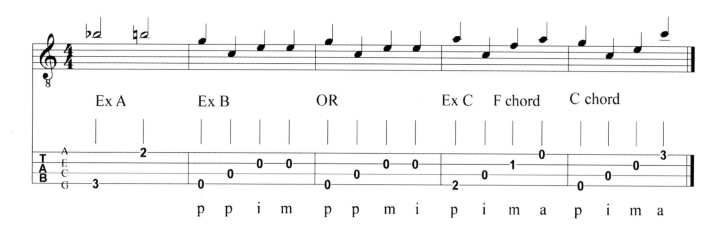

Fingerpicking Starter Kit
Richard Gilewitz

Apply picking pattern to any chord

Arpeggios

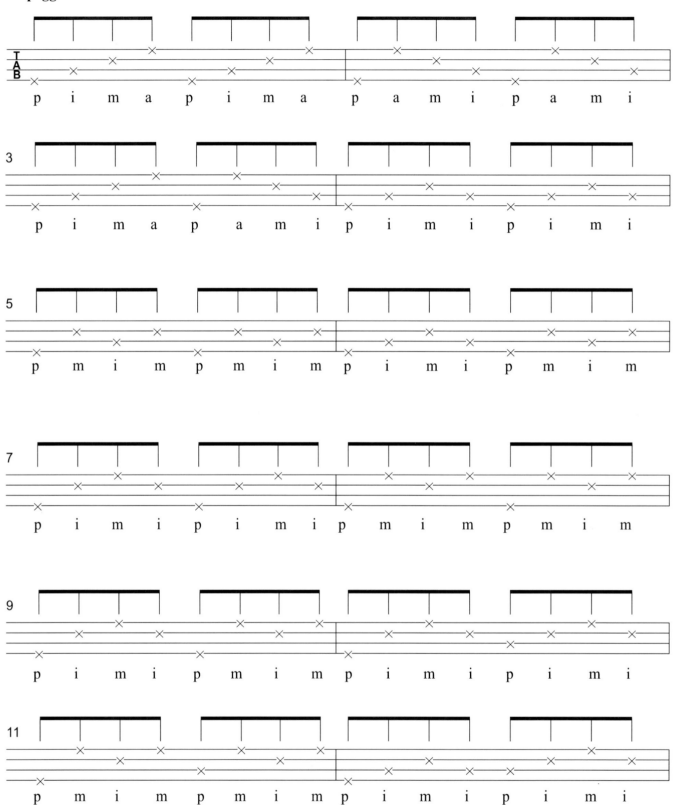

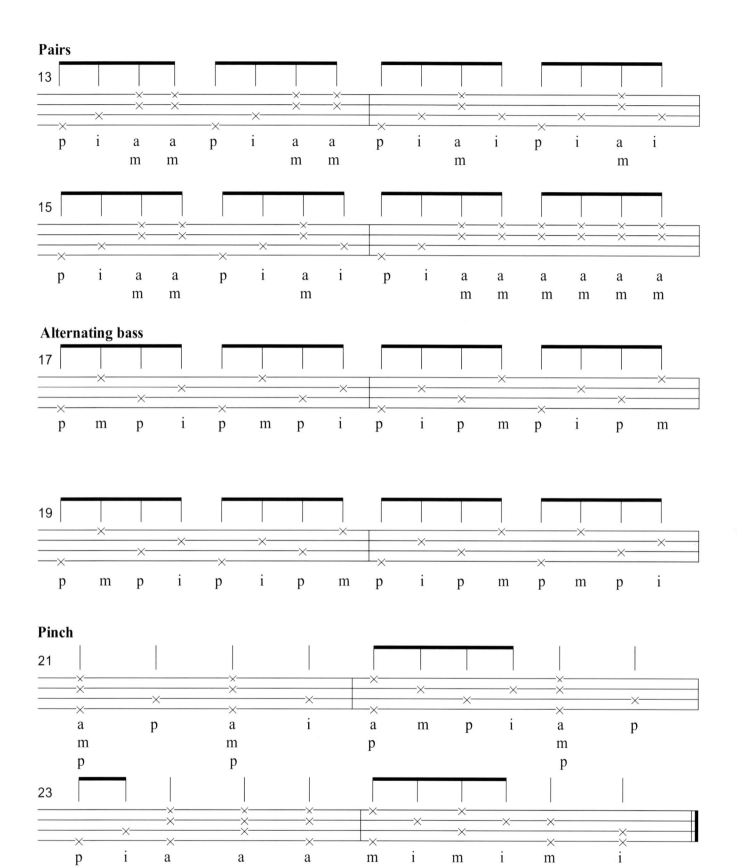

Study Notes

"Twinkle, Twinkle, Little Star"
Key of C

One of the simplest pieces in this collection allows you to engage in the basic art of fingerstyle as you attempt to alternate the plucking fingers back and forth between the index and middle fingers.

Use a metronome to guide you with your timing and see if you can memorize the tune while still using the proper alternating plucking fingers. Although I have made the suggestion to begin with the 'i' or index finger, you may prefer it the other way, beginning with the 'm' or middle finger.

There will be a strong temptation to place your mind on the fretting fingers and neglect the other hand that is plucking. This may lead you to forget to alternate your plucking fingers.

See if you can eventually play the tune with your eyes closed. Investigate the art of visualization as you see in your mind both your left and right hands at work.

Historical Notes

"Twinkle, Twinkle, Little Star" comes from an early 19th-century poem "The Star" by Jane Taylor. This popular English lullaby with lyrics is sung to the tune of the French melody "Ah! vous dirai-je, Maman", published in 1761 and later arranged by several composers including Mozart with Twelve Variations on "Ah vous dirai-je, Maman".

Twinkle, Twinkle, Little Star - Key of C (simple)

Wolfgang Amadeus Mozart
Adapted from "The Star" poem by Jane Taylor

Arranged by Richard Gilewitz

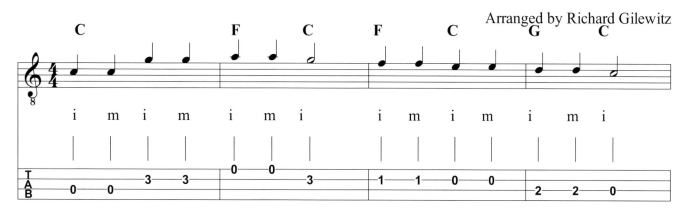

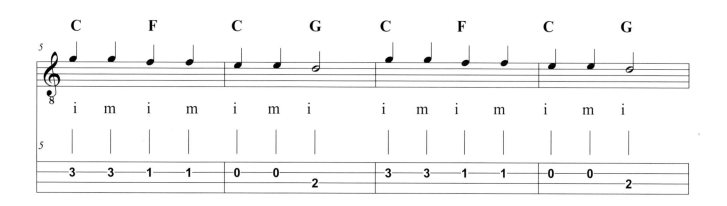

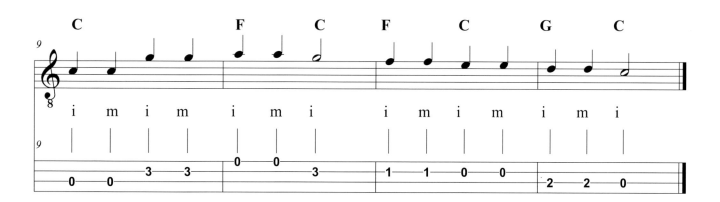

Study Notes

"Bicycle Built for Two"
Key of F

One of the greater challenges with this beautiful and melodic little tune is to use proper restraint in regards to your timing. The music here offers one of the best opportunities to utilize the metronome and learn to wait for the beat.

The introduction of the ring or 'a' finger on string 1 periodically allows for your plucking hand to adapt to the use of this finger in that location.

Try to allow the notes to ring out. You can also apply a technique called vibrato where you give the note a bit of a wiggle with a very rapid, yet minimal, left to right or up or down movement that allows it to sing.

Once again, in regards to plucking hand finger choice, I've simply put in one way to try. Feel free to make your own selections to see what feels comfortable. Once you have made your own choices in mapping out the fingers you have selected lock them in! Allow this to become the way you play the tune. Your hand needs to feel decisive and avoid the conflict of randomization.

Historical Notes

"Daisy Bell (Bicycle Built for Two)" is a popular American song, written in 1892 by Harry Dacre. Inspired by Daisy Greville and a remark from a fellow songwriter in reference to paying import duties twice if Harry had brought a bicycle built for two to America, this tune features the familiar chorus "Daisy, Daisy / Give me your answer, do. / I'm half-crazy / all for the love of you", ending with the words "a bicycle built for two".

Bicycle Built for Two (Daisy Bell)

Harry Dacre

Arranged by Richard Gilewitz

Study Notes

"Grandfather's Clock"
Key of F

This very simple arrangement basically captures the melody of the ballad, "My Grandfather's Clock" and introduces you to the concept of two ideas.

The first is to practice alternating your picking fingers on occasion.

The second is to be sure to wait for the beat and only play the note when the time is right.

This tune is ideal for using the metronome at a reasonable speed to assist you in knowing exactly when the next note should be played.

To keep the fretted note ringing as long as possible, resist the temptation to release the pressure of the finger remaining down on the string until necessary.

Also be mindful not to over press the note and hurt your fingers!

I've left some of the finger selections blank on purpose so that you can begin to make your own choices.

Students have also often asked about the sequence for playing the song. In this case measure 1 has what is called a *pickup note* on beat 4 to lead into the piece. You would then play measures 2-9. Measure 9 is marked with a "1." over it to indicate the 1st ending. You would then go back to the 2nd measure and play through measure 8, skip 9 and go to the 2nd ending marked with a "2." above which appears over measure 10. From that point you play through the rest of the tune.

Historical Notes

"My Grandfather's Clock" was written in 1876 by Harry Clay Work. Told from a grandson's point of view, the song tells the story about a clock that was purchased the morning of his grandfather's birth.

For ninety years, the clock worked perfectly and had to be wound only at the end of each week. The ending lyrics tell the story of when the clock finally stopped.

"But it stopped short — never to go again — when the old man died".

My Grandfather's Clock - Key of F (simple)

Henry Clay Work

Arranged by Richard Gilewitz

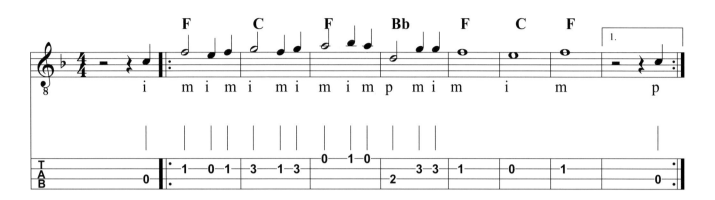

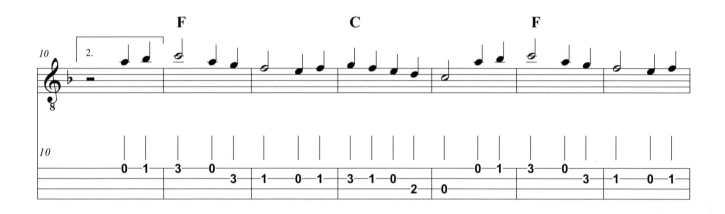

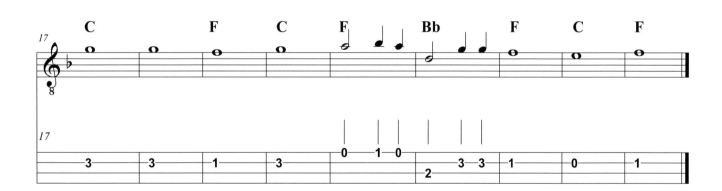

Study Notes

"Oh! Susanna"
Key of C

This rather simple arrangement, which does **not** include the catchy swing rhythm style of playing, is intended to introduce you to the basics of fingerpicking. Try to use your plucking fingers in an alternating fashion as noted so that the fingers almost seem to be walking. As I've mentioned many times before to students, I always try to alternate fingers when possible.

Alternating fingers allows for better hand coordination. Whenever you encounter a piece intended to be played at a rapid pace, you will stand a better chance of not tripping over your fingers. Your playing will be cleaner and you will be more comfortable in not having to guess which finger to use in the next series of notes.

Attempting to play with the same finger twice in a row can severely limit your speed and ability to keep control over the individual power of each strike.

"Oh! Susanna"
Key of D

There are two purposes for learning this arrangement in the key of D. As you practice, your pinky or 4th finger of your fretting hand will gain strength for more complex pieces and longer stretches. You will also learn to place your index or 1st finger of your fretting hand in a bar position at the 2nd fret in order to simulate a capo at that position.

A bit of theory for future reference: If you were to play "Oh! Susanna" in the key of C (one of the versions in this collection) and placed a capo or index finger at the 2nd fret, you would hear the piece in the key of D because of the capo or finger placement. Because of the capo's placement, your fingers would start at the 3rd fret and above.

This is also a handy technique to know if you are already in the key of C and prefer to play in that key when another player joins you and can only play the tune in the key of D.

The suggested plucking fingers noted here are utilizing the thumb or 'p' followed by the index or 'i' fingers in the fashion of a plectrum or flat pick.

Historical Notes

"Oh! Susanna", an American minstrel song by Stephen Foster (1826–1864), was first published in 1848. In 1846, Foster moved to Cincinnati, Ohio, to work as a bookkeeper with his brother's steamship company. While in Cincinnati, Foster penned his first successful songs. Among them was "Oh! Susanna". The tune became an anthem of the California Gold Rush (1848–1849) and the unofficial theme of the Forty-Niners. It is one of the best recognized American songs, blending together a variety of musical traditions. The first two phrases of the melody are based on the major pentatonic scale. Although the opening lyrics refer to "a banjo on my knee", the song takes its beat from the polka, a new European dance style of this period.

Oh! Susanna - Key of C (simple)

Stephen Foster

Arranged by Richard Gilewitz

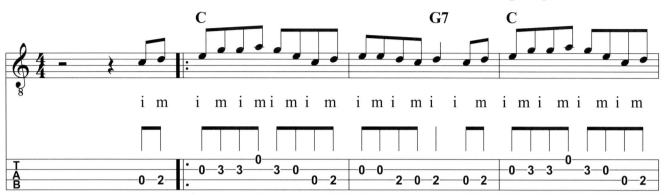

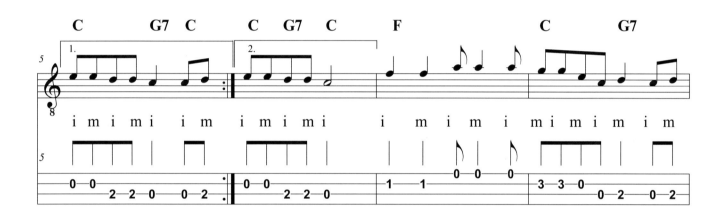

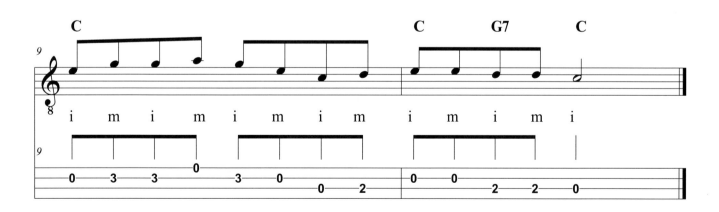

Oh! Susanna - Key of D

Stephen Foster

Arranged by Richard Gilewitz

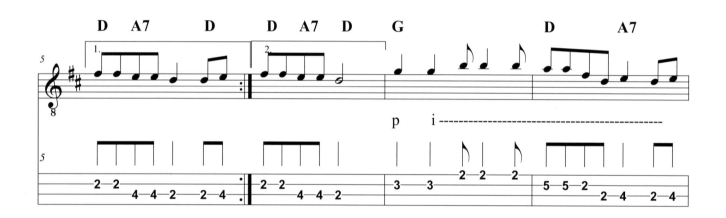

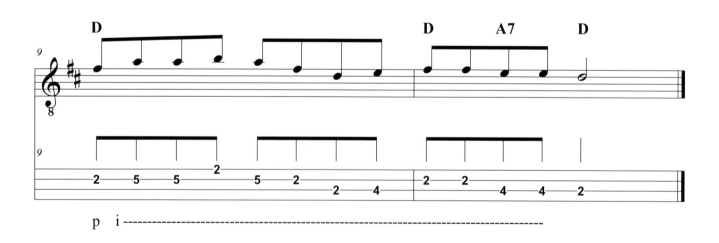

Study Notes

"Auld Lang Syne"
Key of F

This arrangement allows the 'a' or ring finger of the plucking hand to periodically strike string 1. It is also an important finger to use since on a few occasions, two back to back notes are played on the same string. This occurs for the first time in measure 6 and then again in measures 10, 12 and 14. I like to follow the 'a' finger with the 'm' or middle finger to avoid using the same finger twice in a row. Sometimes I will use the 'i' or index followed by the 'm' or middle finger to strike the same string consecutively as you will first discover in measures 2 and 3.

In measures 8 and 16, you will see the 'p' or thumb followed by the 'i' or index finger on the same string. I will often use this approach allowing for the thumb and index to act as a plectrum or flat pick. String 3 is usually the only place I will use this approach.

Feel free once again to make your own plucking finger selections, but remember as I've said before. Once you make your selections try to stick with it almost as if you've programmed your hand to think that this is the only way to play the music. Over time you will instinctively react very quickly with all kinds of movements and substitutions, but this will occur with a lifetime of practice and playing. With a solid system in place for both hands, you will very possibly feel stage fright melt away because it is replaced with decisiveness in your hands which will, in turn, reinforce confidence.

Historical Notes

The tune to which "Auld Lang Syne" is commonly sung as a pentatonic Scottish folk melody, possibly stemmed from a lively dance step in a quicker tempo. Traditionally, it has been adopted by English-speaking countries as a farewell bid to the old year at the stroke of midnight. Non-English speaking countries have adapted the tune for sporting events, bar or restaurant closings, national anthems, and graduations.

The lyrics to "Auld Lang Syne" come from a Scottish poem written by Robert Burns in 1788. The title "Auld Lang Syne" may be translated into Standard English as old long since, long- long ago gone by, or old times. Many think of it as for (the sake of) old times.

Auld Lang Syne - Key of F

Traditional Scottish Folk Melody
Adapted from Robert Burns poem

Arranged by Richard Gilewitz

Study Notes

"Ode to Joy"
Key of F

This lovely little melody allows for a chance to practice pairs of striking fingers, known as double stops, in order to play a harmonized version of the tune with just a pair of strings.

The suggested plucking fingers offers an ideal time to experiment using your middle and ring fingers (m and a) together. It is very important to try and strike the strings with equal power. Too often I have heard players enhance the power of one string over the other, so it's important to keep an ear out for the equal production of the melody.

In measure 4 you have a couple of rapid strikes required and this is a golden opportunity to practice plucking finger substitution. On string 2 you will be alternating your middle and index fingers (m and i) which allows for a much more comfortable situation involving these striking fingers.

The same situation occurs in measures 10 and 11 as the fingers alternate in order to maintain a comfortable coordination of the striking fingers.

Historical Notes

"Ode to Joy", written in 1785 by German poet Friedrich Schiller, is best known for its musical setting by Ludwig van Beethoven. The words are sung during the final moments of Beethoven's Ninth Symphony (completed in 1824), generally by four vocal soloists and a chorus. It is the first example of a major composer using voices in a symphony.

Ode to Joy - Key of F

Ludwig van Beethoven

Arranged by Richard Gilewitz

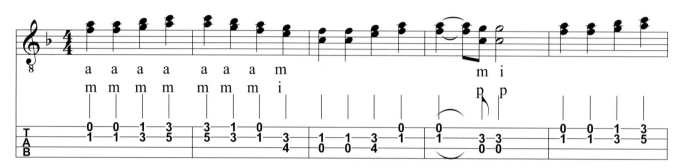

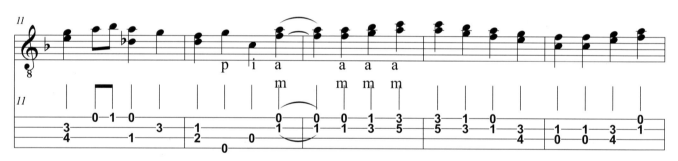

Study Notes

"Silent Night"
Key of C

This piece involves a common occurrence of the arpeggio with the striking fingers. Although there are some pinched notes on occasion, throughout you will notice a succession of single notes in a flowing pattern.

You may notice that in the first measure I take the opportunity to introduce the plucking finger on string 1 with the 'a' or ring finger.

Later in measure 5 you will see a shift downward where the middle finger suddenly moves down to the first string. This allows for the thumb or 'p' finger to play on string 3 which, simply put, felt more comfortable to me when I was mapping the piece out with my fingerings.

Measure 13 would be an ideal time for you to make your own choice and pinch with your thumb and ring finger followed by your middle and then index OR pinch with your thumb and middle finger followed by your index and then thumb again on string 3.

This is a window in on the basic art of mapping out a piece to be played to your own liking.

Historical Notes

The melody was composed by Franz Xaver Gruber, a schoolmaster and organist in the village of Arnsdorf. Father Joseph Mohr brought the words to Gruber, asking him to compose a melody and guitar accompaniment for a Christmas Eve church service. Both Mohr and Gruber performed the carol on the evening of December 24, 1818 at St. Nikola parish church in Oberndorf, Austria. Today, the most frequently sung version is a slow, meditative lullaby. Gruber's original version (particularly in the final strain) was a sprightly, dance-like tune in 6/8 time.

During the Christmas truce of 1914 "Silent Night" was sung simultaneously in English and German by World War I troops. It was the one carol known by the soldiers on both sides of the front line.

Silent Night- Key of C

Franz Xaver Gruber

Arranged by Richard Gilewitz

Study Notes

"Waltzing Matilda"
Key of F

As a favorite tune in this collection, "Waltzing Matilda" is one of the more reasonably challenging pieces to play due to some of the higher reaches that are required in measure 10.

Pay close attention to both the left and right hand fingerings. You may actually use some different fingers that you are more comfortable with, but be sure to always watch for the trap of repeating the same finger on the plucking hand. Whenever possible alternate the picking fingers as required.

Spend some time separating these measures and patch them together for a seamless performance. As with many tunes, this process takes some time and on occasion, quite some time. Here you can say the age-old phrases of "patience is a virtue" and "enjoy the journey!"

Special note: This tune is fun to play with a bit of a swing rhythm, which is a bouncy-type of feel. Wait on adding this element until you get the tune up to speed.

Historical Notes

In 1884, Christina Rutherford MacPherson heard "Bonnie Wood O' Craigielea" a Scottish melody played by the Garrison Artillery band at the Warnambol Races. She adapted it to a zither and played the tune to Banjo Paterson. Working together to fit the words to the melody, the bush ballad "Waltzing Matilda" was created.

In the 1990's, a letter and an original music sheet in Christina's personal handwriting were discovered and presented to the National Library of Australia. These documents provide clear evidence of Christina's contribution to this song. In the letter, written in 1934, Christina describes how she and Australian poet Banjo Paterson came to write "Waltzing Matilda" with her melody and Paterson's lyrics.

Waltzing Matilda

Christian MacPherson (melody)
Banjo Paterson (lyrics)

Arranged by Richard Gilewitz

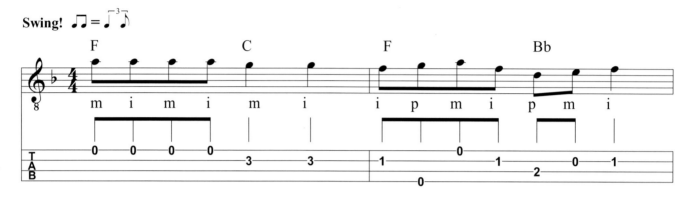

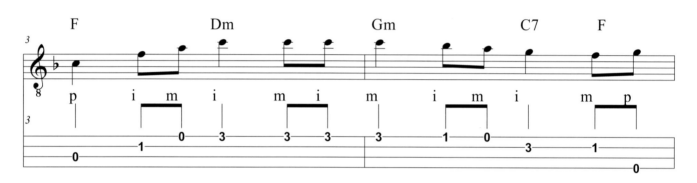

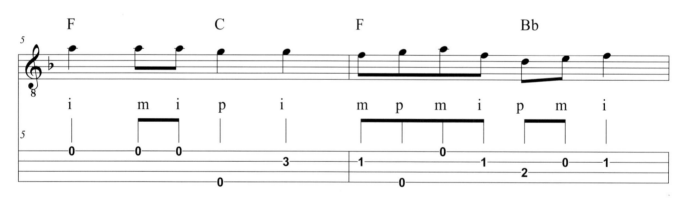

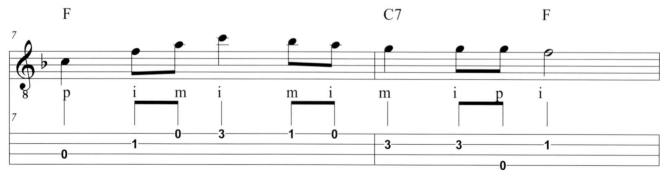

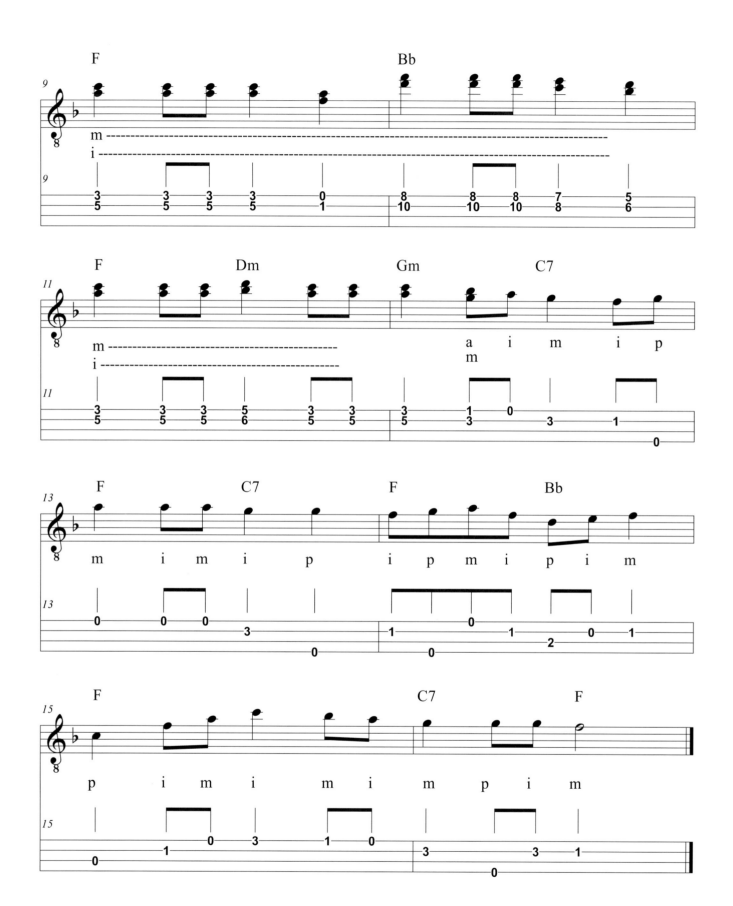

About Richard Gilewitz

Growing up in Cherry Hill, New Jersey and Huntsville, Alabama, Richard embraced diverse artists like The Beatles, Andres Segovia, Kraftwerk, Leo Kottke, J.S. Bach, Arlo Guthrie, John Fahey and Flatt & Scruggs. In those early days, Richard would listen to records of his favorite artists, slowing down the speed to figure out the tunes and emptying out the picks that would fall into the guitar's sound hole. Soaking up the wealth of inspiration supplied by the assorted acts featured at the Renfro Valley festivals, on the "Dr. Demento Radio Show", and "The Midnight Special", Richard took notes on the artists and their tunes. As son of a published writer, recording his observations was natural to Richard and he has never stopped jotting down notes about life on the road, people and places around the globe, or the meanderings of his brain. These bits of paper continue to provide ample material for his performances.

Richard earnestly began honing his skills both as a performer and composer during the late 1970's at the University of Alabama, playing the local coffeehouse circuit while pursing degrees in Computer Science, Mathematics, and Music. During this time he ditched his metal finger picks and concentrated solely on fingerpicking. Following graduation, Richard placed his musical calling in the background and joined the world of flight simulation design, telemetry and satellite systems. The 1980's brought Richard to Florida where he released his first LP recording, *Somewhere In Between.* As the pull of his passion for performing and recording became too compelling, Richard left corporate life to teach, conduct clinics and seminars, and perform full time in a career that has thrust him into an international music arena of nearly four decades. He has gone on to release seven more recordings plus a number of educational materials. In 2014, Richard was challenged to learn ukulele and in turn successfully applied his honed techniques of fingerstyle guitar to this popular instrument. This new endeavor has added a bit more music to the planet by opening a new window for players worldwide who have come to embrace his approach to the ukulele

Tom Ford Photography

Selected Works of Richard Gilewitz

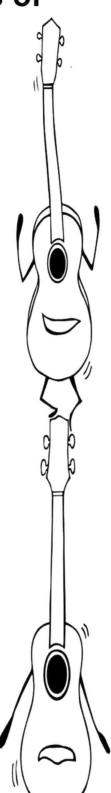

"Echoing Gilewitz"
Duet with Michael Fix
(GillaZilla Records) 2014 - Single

"Minuet for the Backroads"
Duet with Michael Fix
(GillaZilla Records) 2014 - Single

"Mr. Sputnik"
Duet with Michael Fix
(GillaZilla Records) 2014 - Single

"Mr. Sputnik"
(GillaZilla Records) 2013 - Single

"Tater Gun Strut"
(GillaZilla Records) 2013 - Single

Fingerstyle Narratives
(TrueFire) 2012 Software Disc

Slide Guide
(TrueFire) 2012 Software Disc

Tasmania Live
(GillaZilla Records) 2011 - CD

Jump Start - Fingerstyle Guitar
(TrueFire) 2011 Software Disc

Jump Start - Acoustic Guitar
(TrueFire) 2011 Software Disc

Guitar Foundations
(TrueFire) 2009 Software Disc

Strings for a Season
(GillaZilla Records) 2008 - CD

Fingerscapes
(TrueFire) 2008 Software Disc

Richard Gilewitz, Live at Charlotte's
Web
(Mel Bay Publications) 2007 - DVD

Live at 2nd Street Theater
(GillaZilla Records) 2006 - CD

All-Time Favorite Fingerpicking Guitar Tunes, Vol. One
(Mel Bay Publications) 2006 - DVD

Acoustic Fingerstyle Guitar Workshop
(Mel Bay Publications) 2005 - Book, CD, DVD

Master Anthology of Fingerstyle Guitar Solos, Vol. 3
(Mel Bay Publications) 2005 - Book, CD

Thumbsing
(GillaZilla Records) 2004 - CD

All Star Guitar Night
(Mel Bay Publications) 2002 DVD

Fingerstyle Guitar Selections
(GillaZilla Music) 2002 - Book

Dirt To Dust
(mp3.com compilation) 2001

Richard Gilewitz Music and Instruction for Fingerstyle
Guitar
(Peavey Electronics) 2000 Video

The Music of David Walbert
(GillaZilla Records) 2000 - CD

Synapse Collapse
(GillaZilla Records) 1997 - CD

Performance Video
(Alligator Alley Productions) 1996 - [out of print]

Instructional Video
(Alligator Alley Productions) 1995 - [out of print]

Voluntary Solitary
(GillaZilla Records) 1994 - CD

The Richard Gilewitz Songbook
(Armadillo Press) 1993 – Book (out of print)

Somewhere In Between
(Hacker Backer Records) 1992 - Vinyl [out of print]

Contact Information:
Richard Gilewitz c/o GillaZilla Music
PO Box 3023
Inverness FL 34451 USA
www.richardgilewitz.com
Expand your Ukulele Adventure at GillaCamp
www.gillacamp.com

Let's Thank Those on the Team

While working on this book, I attempted to cover every detail and not let a single error slip through the cracks along the way. This attention to detail required a battery of folks who were willing to add their ears and eyes to the creation of this book. Now I know why these special thanks segments are tucked away in the back of the book. It's the author's humble way of admitting that it took a dedicated team to pull off a project. If I have missed a crew member, I apologize in advance and ask you not to pelt me with fruit the next time I'm on stage playing my ukulele.

There is no order of thanks because it was truly a team effort with possibly the laziest man (me) at the helm! Let me start with a hats-off to Bill Bay of Mel Bay Publications for giving me the opportunity to write this book. Thanks for believing in me and letting me pass along my passion for teaching my fingerstyle techniques to ukulele players and for continuing to laugh at my jokes.

My own guitar instructor for over 40 years, David Walbert, was magnificent in detailing every little musical nuance that caught his eye, whether it was a questionable note value, inaccurate melody, missing tied note, improper chord or key and general sense of accuracy within the music.

Yvonne Desrosiers was exceptional as well with her instant communication and turnaround time with most of the charts, study note observations, guidance and friendship throughout the project.

Karlo Senasi was invaluable in converting the music files to Finale. Both Karlo and Yvonne stuck with me even during those "just one more little change" moments that popped up at the last minute.

Tim May, a good friend and award-winning fellow player, was very kind and forthcoming offering suggestions across the board prior to the assembly of all the content. Extra special thanks to Tim Roberts of Waterknot Music Nashville for the mixing and mastering of the tunes.

A few of my beginner ukulele students were also keen to assist in realistically sharing their insights. This real-time guidance helped tremendously in keeping me within the proper bounds, as I realized that throwing in a "Bach Fugue" into the mix would not work. So a big shout out to Connie Wendt, Clayton Long, Juliet Mattingly, Ron Brannan, and several members from my ukulele class at Master the Possibilities at the Top of the World.

Thanks as well to my sponsors. I could not have a better lineup of supporters than D'Addario Strings, Shubb Capos, Audio-Technica Microphones, and LR Baggs pickups. Extra special kudos go out to Bob Rohan for the Gilewitz cartoon and Perry Harper for her photo retouching and ukulele character illustrations. Photo credits to Tom Ford and Beverly Gilewitz.

Big thanks to my friend and luthier, Charlie Jirousek of Arrowhead Music, for the hand-crafted ukulele that was built from Peruvian walnut (aged from 1974) and topped off with a Wooly Mammoth fossil inlay in the headstock.

And of course my wife, Beverly, who edited and packaged all the material in a sensible and readable form and sequence, provided guidance, motivation, and support throughout and prevented this project from looking like it came out of a yard sale!